# Instant IntroJs

Learn how to work with the IntroJs library to create useful, step-by-step help and introductions for websites and applications

**Ehsan Arasteh**

**Afshin Mehrabani**

PUBLISHING

BIRMINGHAM - MUMBAI

# Instant IntroJs

First published: September 2013

Production Reference: 1230913

Published by Packt Publishing Ltd.
Livery Place
35 Livery Street
Birmingham B3 2PB, UK.

ISBN 978-1-78328-251-7

www.packtpub.com

# Credits

**Authors**

Ehsan Arasteh

Afshin Mehrabani

**Reviewers**

Greg Babula

Mustafa Serhat Dündar

**Acquisition Editors**

Martin Bell

Rebecca Youe

**Commissioning Editor**

Sruthi Kutty

**Technical Editors**

Amit Ramadas

Rohit Kumar Singh

**Copy Editors**

Alfida Paiva

Kirti Pai

**Project Coordinator**

Amigya Khurana

**Proofreader**

Clyde Jenkins

**Production Coordinator**

Nilesh R. Mohite

**Cover Work**

Nilesh R. Mohite

**Cover Image**

Valentina D'silva

# About the Authors

**Ehsan Arasteh** currently works as the CTO and Software Architect at Yaraholding, a Tehran-based interactive agency and web development company. He has nine years experience in development with several languages, such as ASP.NET, C#, Java, PHP, and Python. He has also worked on banking projects, professional web applications, and so on.

He is also the CEO of Usablica; a company that makes open source applications, such as IntroJs and Magnet.

He started teaching C and C++ to high school students at the age of fourteen. He grew up with programming and started his professional life with his first official project when he was sixteen. It was his starting point in the official programming community. Since then, he has done a lot of projects as a developer, analyzer, consultant, architect, and project manager. He also came back to Academic Systems as an instructor in a game development institute, but he says, "Nothing is replaceable with coding".

I would like to thank my amazing wife, for her support and resilience. Without her help, I couldn't have done this important job.

**Afshin Mehrabani** is a 21-year old software engineer and an open source programmer. He started programming and web development with PHP when he was 12 years old. Later, he entered the Iran Technical & Vocational Training Organization. He received the gold medal in a country-wide competition on web development, and he also became a member of the Iran's National Elites Foundation by producing a variety of new programming ideas.

He was a software engineer at the Tehran Stock Exchange and he is already the head of the web development team in the Yara Company. He co-founded the Usablica team in early 2012 to develop and produce usable applications. Afshin is the author of IntroJs, WideArea, Flood.js, and other open source projects.

Also, he is contributing to Socket.IO, Engine.IO, and other open source projects. His interests are in creating and contributing to open source applications, writing programming articles, and challenging himself with new programming technologies.

He has already written different articles about JavaScript, NodeJs, HTML5, and MongoDB, which are published on different academic websites. Afshin has five years experience with PHP, Python, C#, JavaScript, HTML5, and NodeJs in many financial and stock trading projects.

I would like to thank my parents and my lovely sister, Parvin, for their support, which gave me the power to keep going.

Also, I'd like to thank my friends in the Usablica team for their efforts in developing and contributing to the IntroJs library. I would also like to thank my special friends Ehsan Arasteh and Amir Vahid Roudsari, who helped me to prepare and complete this book.

# About the Reviewers

**Greg Babula** is a client-side developer with over a decade of experience. He loves crafting rich user experiences and interfaces while maintaining a high quality of clean and structured frontend code.

Currently, Greg is a co-lead developer, leading all frontend efforts of OurGroup, INC. In the past, he has helped lead projects for clients, such as AMTRAK, Fidelity, White House ONDCP, Janssen, Auxilium, and Columbia University.

> I would like to thank my wife Agnieszka for supporting me and my dreams.

**Mustafa Serhat Dündar** is the system administrator of Ondokuz Mayis University/Distance Education Center, and is experienced in Moodle, Adobe Connect, MySQL, Oracle 11g, Python, and PHP. He is also a GNU fan, and enjoys contributing to open source projects.

Mustafa Serhat Dündar is working at the Ondokuz Mayis University/Distance Education Center. He follows the path of two amazing people and keeps learning a lot from them, Sönmez Pamuk, Ph.D. and Recai Oktas, Ph.D.

> I'm grateful to my father Erhan Dündar, my mother Fatma Dündar, and my dear girlfriend Yesim Kuran for their endless support.

# www.packtpub.com

## Support files, eBooks, discount offers and more

You might want to visit www.packtpub.com for support files and downloads related to your book.

Did you know that Packt offers eBook versions of every book published, with PDF and ePub files available? You can upgrade to the eBook version at www.packtpub.com and as a print book customer, you are entitled to a discount on the eBook copy. Get in touch with us at service@packtpub.com for more details.

At www.packtpub.com, you can also read a collection of free technical articles, sign up for a range of free newsletters and receive exclusive discounts and offers on Packt books and eBooks.

# packtlib.packtpub.com

Do you need instant solutions to your IT questions? PacktLib is Packt's online digital book library. Here, you can access, read and search across Packt's entire library of books.

## Why Subscribe?

- ✦ Fully searchable across every book published by Packt
- ✦ Copy and paste, print and bookmark content
- ✦ On demand and accessible via web browser

## Free Access for Packt account holders

If you have an account with Packt at www.packtpub.com, you can use this to access PacktLib today and view nine entirely free books. Simply use your login credentials for immediate access.

# Table of Contents

# Instant IntroJs

Welcome to the *Instant IntroJs*. This book has been especially created to provide you with all the information that you need to get set up with IntroJs. You will learn the basics of IntroJs, get started with building your first step-by-step introduction, and discover some tips.

This document contains the following sections:

*So, what is IntroJs?* helps you find out out what IntroJs actually is, and what you can do with it.

*Installation* teaches how to download and install IntroJs with minimum fuss, and then set it up so that you can use it as soon as possible.

*Quick start* shows you how to perform one of the core tasks of IntroJs—creating basic introductions. Follow the steps to create your own basic introduction, which will be the basis of most of your work in IntroJs.

*Top 7 features you need to know about* teaches how to perform some tasks with the most important features of IntroJs. By the end of this section, you will be able to customize IntroJs with your preferred stylesheet, use IntroJs options and public APIs, change button labels or localize them with your language, use IntroJs with Rails, PHP Yii, and other frameworks, use IntroJs callback functions and events, build and minify the library, define introductions with JSON configurations, and also create a multipage introduction or help.

*People and places you should get to know* provides you with many useful links to the project pages and forums, as well as a number of helpful articles, tutorials, samples, blogs, and the Twitter feeds of IntroJs super contributors. This is because every open source project is centered around a community.

# So, what is IntroJs?

Web developers must realize that it is important that their websites are self-explanatory. Website navigation should be obvious. Users do not expect to spend too much time to find out how to use a website. What if you need to explain your website to your visitors? To achieve these goals, designing an info-graphic chart would be one of the best approaches.

Users are the most important assets, and it is vital to inform them about new changes in your website. It is always easier to lose a significant number of users by not introducing them to updates and changes rather than attracting them. So how are you going to inform them about these changes? Surely, you are looking for the best and the shortest way to avoid wasting time and energy.

**IntroJs** is a library that helps to inform users about new changes and indicates the new version's functionality. When a customer or a user visits a website, it is vital to show them the website's functions and new updates to improve user interaction, performance, and ability to work with the website in an easier and faster manner. Even a big feature might be ignored by a visitor just because of the complications. Hence, showing the website features clearly could have the biggest effect on the failure or success of the website.

To improve the users' knowledge while filling a huge form and to speed this process, it's better to give them more information about it. IntroJs is a library that lets the developers break their website into highlighted segments to help customers and users use their website in a better way. By using this library, they can create a step-by-step introduction to show the website's features, and also inform users about new changes.

## Usages

IntroJs could be used in several situations in order to make things easy to understand and useful for audiences. IntroJs is basically used for the following:

+ Introducing a part to the user
+ Creating a step-by-step introduction
+ Creating a multipage introduction
+ Showing new updates and changes to the user

IntroJs was developed and designed with JavaScript and CSS3. To use IntroJs, both JavaScript and CSS files need to be included in the page, and IntroJs methods need to be called. There is no dependence between IntroJs and other libraries, and there is no need to use any other libraries on the page.

## Features

IntroJs is a lightweight, open source, and easy-to-use library with an active community of users and developers. Some of the notable features are as follows:

+ Small size (4 KB JavaScript and 2 KB CSS)
+ Easy to use
+ Pure JavaScript and CSS
+ No dependence with other libraries
+ Compatible with mobile and tablet devices
+ Compatible with older browsers
+ Free and open source
+ MIT license

# Installation

In this section, we will cover the following points:

◆   What are the IntroJs requirements?

◆   How to download?

◆   How to install?

IntroJs is a client-side library, which means all routines and events manage and execute on the client environment. All installation and running steps are related to client segments, and there is no requirement to install it on the server.

There are four simple steps to install and run IntroJs.

## Step 1 – requirements

As mentioned before, to run IntroJs, there is no need to install anything on the server, and all the work is on the client side; all you need is just a web browser.

To run IntroJs, you need to have one of the following web browsers:

◆   IE 8 or higher

◆   Firefox 20 or higher

◆   Google Chrome 26 or higher

◆   Safari 5.1 or higher

◆   Opera 12.1 or higher

There are some requirements for mobile or tablet browsers as well:

◆   iOS Safari 3.2 or higher

◆   Opera Mini 5.0-0.7 or higher

◆   Android Browser 2.1 or higher

◆   BlackBerry Browser 7.0 or higher

## Step 2 – downloading JavaScript and CSS

To install and run IntroJs, download the latest version. All necessary files of each version should be sorted in a separated folder.

The GitHub page for IntroJs is the simplest and easiest way to download the latest version, which is available on `https://github.com/usablica/intro.js/tags`.

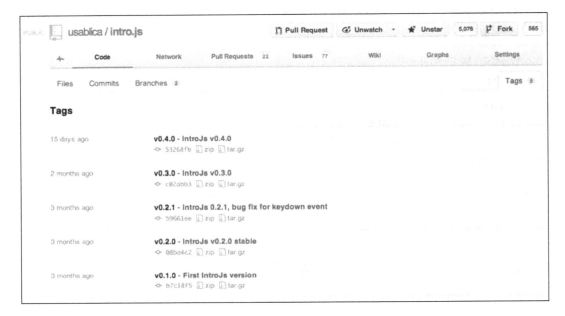

As the screenshot indicates, all versions are available in the `.zip` and `tar.gz` formats. Download the latest version. At the time of writing this book, the latest available version was 0.4.0.

Also, an unstable version is available at `https://github.com/usablica/intro.js/archive/master.zip`.

Note that the version under development may have some problems or bugs. It is only available for introducing the latest features, updates, and changes in the library; it won't be useful for production.

After download, extract the compressed file. It usually includes the following files and directories:

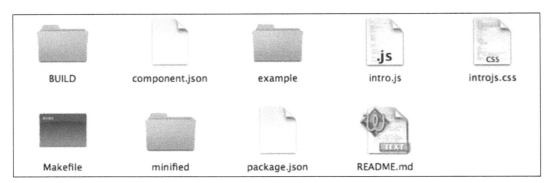

The following is an explanation for a few of these:

+ The `BUILD` folder is useful to build and make production files
+ The `example` folder includes some samples of how to use IntroJs
+ The `minified` folder contains the minified files that you need during production
+ The `intro.js` and `introjs.css` files are the library's main files useful for development or fixing bugs (they are not recommended for production; for production purpose, use minified files)
+ Also, `component.json` and `package.json` are package-management tools for configuration purposes

## Step 3 – configuration

IntroJs can run on any HTML page by performing the following steps.

The `intro.min.js` and `intro.min.css` files are the two main files for installation that are available in the minified folder. These two files are made for the production environment. They are available in the compressed mode, and all the extra comments and descriptions have been removed from them.

There are two methods to call IntroJs files. However, it is possible to use either way, but to achieve higher speed and accuracy, the second method has been approached.

### Using the <script> tag

To use the `<script>` tag, include the following JavaScript and CSS files in the HTML document:

```
<!-- Add IntroJs -->
<script type="text/javascript"src="intro.min.js"></script>
<!-- Add IntroJs styles -->
<linkhref="introjs.min.css"rel="stylesheet">
```

### AMD and CommonJs

Another useful feature of IntroJs is its compatibility with AMD and CommonJs patterns. It is possible to call JavaScript and CSS files using these patterns, and it doesn't need to use the `<script>` tag. Also, by using this, it would be possible to call JavaScript and CSS files asynchronously.

This approach increases the document's loading speed, and also, the web page won't block while loading. As mentioned before, this method has been recommended instead of the other one.

```
require(["intro"], function(introJs) {
    //This function is called when intro.js is loaded.
    //Hence, you can write `introJs().start();` here
});
```

This code is written using the RequireJs library. By using this method, the scope or closure of the IntroJs program will be determined. Also, the request to load the file will be sent asynchronously, and it won't wait for the flow of calling to be finished. Moreover, it also increases the loading speed.

To use this feature, you need to have one of the following libraries in your page:

+ RequireJs
+ curl
+ LSJS
+ Dojo 1.7 or higher

Also, by using this method, it is possible to call `introjs.css`. However, due to the problems that this method can cause in different browsers, it is not recommended to be used, and the `<link>` tag has been preferred to call CSS files instead.

## And that's it

By this point, you should have a working installation of IntroJs; you are now free to play around and discover more about it.

# Quick start

In this section, the following subjects will be discussed:

+ Settings
+ Creating a new example

Do you need to create an introduction page using IntroJs? Two simple steps to do this are explained in this section.

## Step 1 – defining elements

Elements could be defined with the following two approaches:

+ Using element attributes
+ Using JavaScript objects (JSON)

### Using element attributes

With this approach, you can easily set up and define your first introduction. For setting up the introduction with attributes, add some custom attributes that want to be a part of the story to the elements. `data-intro` and `data-step` make it possible to add some text or caption to the highlighted element or to change the position of the tool tip. To achieve these, perform the steps outlined in this section.

### The data-intro attribute

It is possible to have a tool tip for each introduction's step, which gives brief information about it to the user. The `data-intro` attribute defines the tool tip text when the element gets highlighted, for example:

```
<a href='http://google.com/' data-intro='Hello step one!'>I'm a link</
a>
```

The preceding example generates a `Hello step one!` tool tip text.

### The data-step attribute

The `data-step` attribute sets the priority for each step with a number in the introduction, for example:

```
<a href='http://google.com/' data-intro='Hello step one!' data-
step='1'>Link One</a>
<a href='http://yahoo.com/' data-intro='Hello step two!' data-
step='2'>Link Two</a>
```

In this example, we have two elements in the introduction with different priorities or `data-step` attributes. When the introduction starts, first of all, the value of `Link One` is highlighted before that of `Link Two` due to a higher priority of `data-step`. Also, it is possible to change the priority after adding some other elements with different `data-step` attributes.

### The data-position attribute

The `data-position` attribute makes it possible to set the tool tip box's position. However, it is an optional attribute, but it lets us set the proper position of tool tip boxes. By default, the position of the tool tip boxes is set to be at the bottom of the highlighted element. However, it is possible to change it with the `data-position` attribute. The `data-position` attribute can get `top`, `bottom`, `left`, or `right` values, for example:

```
<a href='http://google.com/' data-intro='Hello step one!' data-
step='1' data-position='right'>Link One</a>
```

The preceding example generates the `Hello step one!` tool tip text, and the tool tip box will appear on the right-hand side.

## Using JavaScript objects (JSON)

A JavaScript object or JSON is another way to define the introduction. There is no difference between this approach and element attributes. However, it is a clear way to generate the introduction programmatically.

IntroJs has a method called `setOptions`, and it gives us the ability to set some options to the library. One of these options is the `steps` property, which holds all the steps of the introduction in an array.

First of all, create an instance of `introJS`. Then, call `setOptions` (or `setOption`) to set all the steps. Now, all we need is to create an array of the steps in our introduction. Each step and all the properties hold an object, which includes the following properties:

* `element`: This defines the target element of the introduction and is a CSS selector
* `intro`: This includes the text of the tool tip box
* `step`: This includes a number to set each step's priority
* `position`: This represents the position of the tool tip box, which can be `top`, `bottom`, `right`, or `left`

The following code is an example of a step:

```
{
    element:'#step2',
    intro:"Ok, wasn't that fun?",
    position:'right'
}
```

A complete example of all the steps is as follows:

```
var intro =introJs();
        intro.setOptions({
          steps: [
          {
            element:'#step1',
            intro:"This is a tooltip."
          },
          {
            element:'#step2',
            intro:"Ok, wasn't that fun?",
            position:'right'
          },
          {
            element:'#step3',
            intro:'More features, more fun.',
            position:'left'
          }
        ]
});
```

In the preceding example, we created an instance of `introJS` and defined three steps of the introduction.

## Step 2 – calling the start() method

We are almost done! Calling the `start()` method from the `introJS` instance is the final step to create the introduction.

IntroJs has a constructor method that creates an instance in the library and sets all options to it. The constructor method can get one parameter, which defines the farm of the introduction, for example, running the introduction for the whole page or only for a specific element or container.

An example for the whole page is as follows:

```
var instance = introJs(); //without selector, start introduction for
whole page
```

And an example for a specific container is as follows:

```
var instance = introJs("#intro-farm"); //start introduction for
element id='intro-farm'
```

In the preceding examples, we created two instances of `introJS`, the first one without a specific element and the second one with `#intro-farm`. Now we have an instance of `introJS`, and all we need is to call the `start()` method.

```
instance.start();
```

After calling the `start()` method, the introduction starts. To define steps with a JavaScript object, we need to call `setOptions()` first, and then call the `start()` method.

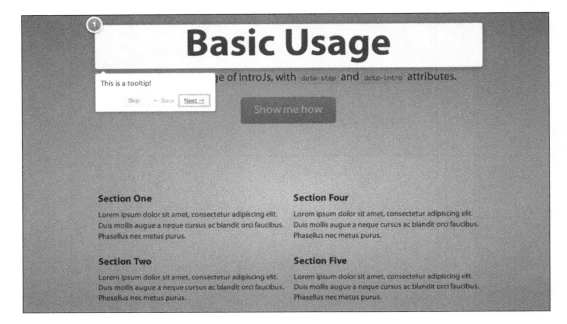

## Hello World

Alright, now let's create our first introduction using the basic features of IntroJs. First, create your `hello-world.html` file as follows:

```
<!DOCTYPE html>
<html lang="en">
<head>
<meta charset="utf-8">
<title>IntroJS-Hello World</title>
<!-- Add IntroJs styles -->
<link href="introjs.css" rel="stylesheet">
</head>
<body>
<div>
<h1 >Basic Usage</span></h1>
<p class="lead" data-step="4" data-intro="Another step.">This is the
basic
usage of IntroJs, with <code>data-step</code> and <code>data-intro</
code> attributes.
</p>
<a class="btnbtn-large btn-success" href="javascript:void(0);"
onclick="javascript:introJs().start();">Start</a>
</div>
```

```
<div>
<div>
<h4 data-step="1" data-intro="This is a tooltip!">Section One</h4>
<p>Loremipsum dolor sitamet, consecteturadipiscingelit.
Duismollisaugue a nequecursus ac blanditorcifaucibus.
Phasellusnecmetuspurus.</p>
<h4 data-step="2" data-intro="This is a tooltip!">Section Two</h4>
<p>Loremipsum dolor sitamet, consecteturadipiscingelit.
Duismollisaugue a nequecursus ac blanditorcifaucibus.
Phasellusnecmetuspurus.</p>
<h4 data-step="3" data-intro="This is a tooltip!">Section Three</h4>
<p>Loremipsum dolor sitamet, consecteturadipiscingelit.
Duismollisaugue a nequecursus ac blanditorcifaucibus.
Phasellusnecmetuspurus.</p>
</div>
</div>
</div>
<script type="text/javascript" src="intro.js"></script>
</body>
</html>
```

Open `hello-world.html` in the browser. It's the first introduction using the IntroJs library.

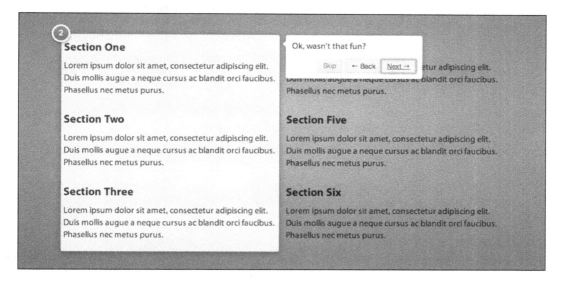

## How it works

You have created the first introduction; it was easy and simple. First of all, include JavaScript and CSS files on the page. Then, add three `<h4>` elements with the `data-step` attribute to the code. Finally, in the `<a>` tag's `onClick` event, call the `start()` function from IntroJs.

Other features of IntroJs will be discussed in the next section.

# Top 7 features you need to know about

IntroJs has a robust and complete API, which gives you the ability to customize and change the library with your preferred settings.

In this section the following subjects will be discussed:

+ Options
+ API
+ Customizing CSS files
+ Integrating IntroJs with other frameworks
+ Localization and the Right to Left version
+ Build
+ Multipaging

You have already learned the basic features of IntroJs. In this section, all library features will be covered. Also, the way to customize the IntroJs style to the style the developer is looking for will be discussed. Later on, the way to localize the library for different languages will be reviewed, and finally, with some examples, you will learn how to integrate IntroJs with other frameworks.

## Options

There are some default options available in IntroJs to configure the library, such as the **Next**, **Back**, and **Done** button label in the tool tip box or the default position of tool tips.

In this section, all options of IntroJs, and in the following sections, some other methods to alter these options and the set preferred values are available.

### steps

To define steps manually using JSON configuration, the `steps` property is useful. In the *Quick start* section, we discussed this option, which has a JavaScript Object (JSON) type.

### nextLabel

The `nextLabel` option holds the text to be displayed in the tool tip box of the **Next** button. The type of this option is `string` and its default value is **Next** →.

## prevLabel

The `prevLabel` option saves the text to be displayed in the tool tip box of the **Back** button. Its type is `string` and its default value is **← Back**.

## skipLabel

The `skipLabel` option is used to set the **Skip** button text in the tool tip box. The type of this option is `string` and **Skip** is its default value.

## doneLabel

The `doneLabel` option holds the **Done** button's text in the tool tip box. When the user reaches the last step of the introduction, this button will appear. Also, its type is `string` and its default value is **Done**.

## tooltipPosition

The `tooltipPosition` option is used to hold the default position of the tool tip boxes in the introduction. The default value of this option is `bottom`, and it means that all tool tip boxes will appear at the bottom of the highlighted area that is available in the introduction. Also, possible values for this option are `top`, `bottom`, `right`, and `left`.

## exitOnEsc

The `exitOnEsc` option is a `true` or `false` option that defines if the user can exit the introduction by using the *Esc* key or not. The type of this option is `boolean` and its possible values are true and false, which by default is set to `true`. By setting it to `false`, *Esc* will be disabled.

## exitOnOverlayClick

The `exitOnOverlayClick` option is a true or false option that is useful to define if the user can exit the introduction by clicking on the overlay layer (dark background in the introduction) in the introduction or not. The type of this option is `boolean` and its possible values are `true` or `false`, which by default is set to `true`.

## showStepNumbers

The `showStepNumbers` option is another `true` or `false` option. By setting it to true, the number of each step will be shown on the top-right side of the highlighted area. Its possible values are `true` or `false` and its default value is `true`.

## API

IntroJs includes functions that let the user to control and change the execution of the introduction. For example, it is possible to make a decision for an unexpected event that happens during execution, or to change the introduction routine according to user interactions. Later on, all available APIs in IntroJs until the time of writing this book will be explained. However, these functions will extend and develop in the future. IntroJs includes these API functions:

- `start`
- `goToStep`
- `exit`
- `setOption`
- `setOptions`
- `oncomplete`
- `onexit`
- `onchange`
- `onbeforechange`

### introJs.start()

As mentioned before, `introJs.start()` is the main function of IntroJs that lets the user to start the introduction for specified elements and get an instance of the `introJS` class. The introduction will start from the first step in specified elements.

This function has no arguments and also returns an instance of the `introJS` class.

### introJs.goToStep(stepNo)

Jump to the specific step of the introduction by using this function. As it is clear, introductions always start from the first step; however, it is possible to change the configuration by using this function. The `goToStep` function has an integer argument that accepts the number of the step in the introduction.

```
introJs().goToStep(2).start(); //starts introduction from step 2
```

As the example indicates, first, the default configuration changed by using the `goToStep` function from 1 to 2, and then the `start()` function will be called. Hence, the introduction will start from the second step.

Finally, this function will return the `introJS` class's instance.

# introJs.exit()

The `introJS.exit()` function lets the user exit and close the running introduction. By default, the introduction ends when the user clicks on the **Done** button or goes to the last step of the introduction.

```
introJs().exit()
```

As it shows, the `exit()` function doesn't have any arguments and returns an instance of `introJS`.

# introJs.setOption(option, value)

As mentioned before, IntroJs has some default options that can be changed by using the `setOption` method. This function has two arguments. The first one is useful to specify the option name and the second one is to set the value.

```
introJs().setOption("nextLabel", "Go Next");
```

In the preceding example, `nextLabel` sets to `Go Next`. Also, it is possible to change other options by using the `setOption` method.

# introJs.setOptions(options)

It is possible to change an option using the `setOption` method. However, to change more than one option at once, it is possible to use `setOptions` instead. The `setOptions` method accepts different options and values in the JSON format.

```
introJs().setOptions({ skipLabel: "Exit", tooltipPosition: "right" });
```

In the preceding example, two options are set at the same time by using JSON and the `setOptions` method.

# introJs.oncomplete(providedCallback)

The `oncomplete` event is raised when the introduction ends. If a function passes as an `oncomplete` method, it will be called by the library after the introduction ends.

```
introJs().oncomplete(function() {
  alert("end of introduction");
});
```

In this example, after the introduction ends, the anonymous function that is passed to the `oncomplete` method will be called and alerted with the **end of introduction** message.

### introJs.onexit(providedCallback)

As mentioned before, the user can exit the running introduction using the *Esc* key or by clicking on the dark area in the introduction. The `onexit` event notices when the user exits from the introduction. This function accepts one argument and returns the instance of running `introJS`.

```
introJs().onexit(function() {
  alert("exit of introduction");
});
```

In the preceding example, we passed an anonymous function to the `onexit` method with an `alert()` statement. If the user exits the introduction, the anonymous function will be called and an alert with the message **exit of introduction** will appear.

### introJs.onchange(providedCallback)

The `onchange` event is raised in each step of the introduction. This method is useful to inform when each step of introduction is completed.

```
introJs().onchange(function(targetElement) {
  alert("new step");
});
```

You can define an argument for an anonymous function (`targetElement` in the preceding example), and when the function is called, you can access the current target element that is highlighted in the introduction with that argument. In the preceding example, when each introduction's step ends, an alert with the **new step** message will appear.

### introJs.onbeforechange(providedCallback)

Sometimes, you may need to do something before each step of introduction. Consider that you need to do an Ajax call before the user goes to a step of the introduction; you can do this with the `onbeforechange` event.

```
introJs().onbeforechange(function(targetElement) {
  alert("before new step");
});
```

We can also define an argument for an anonymous function (`targetElement` in the preceding example), and when this function is called, the argument gets some information about the currently highlighted element in the introduction. So using that argument, you can know which step of the introduction will be highlighted or what's the type of target element and more.

In the preceding example, an alert with the message **before new step** will appear before highlighting each step of the introduction.

# Method chaining

**Method chaining** is one of the most useful features of IntroJs. This method calls functions after each other continuously.

Consider that you need to call two or three methods to do an action. For example, set an option, set a callback event, and then call a `start()` method to start the introduction. There are two different ways to achieve this goal. First, create an instance of the class and hold it in a variable, and then call other functions using that variable. Second, use method chaining. In IntroJs, you call functions one after another, just like a chain.

Here you can see the traditional usage of classes and functions:

```
//first of all, create an instance of IntroJs and hold it in a
variable
varmyIntro = introJs();

//change skipLabel and tooltipPosition
myIntro.setOptions({ skipLabel: "Exit", tooltipPosition: "right" });

//set function to call in onchange
myIntro.onchange(function(targetElement) {
  alert("new step");
});

//set funtion to call in onexit
myIntro.onexit(function() {
  alert("exit of introduction");
});

//finally start the introduction
myIntro.start();
```

This consists of a lot of lines and code and makes it too complicated. It is much better to change it as shown in the following code snippet:

```
introJs.setOptions({ skipLabel: "Exit", tooltipPosition: "right" })
.onchange(function(targetElement) {
  alert("new step");
})
.onexit(function() {
  alert("exit of introduction");
})
.start();
```

As the preceding code snippet shows, we called each function one after another. Actually, all functions of IntroJs return an instance of `introJS`; hence, you don't need to hold the instance in a separated variable and then use it.

[  To find more about method chaining, use the following link:
`http://en.wikipedia.org/wiki/Method_chaining`. ]

## Integrating IntroJs with other frameworks

We can integrate a server-side framework with IntroJs. It helps to use IntroJs in your server-side code and also to provide more control on IntroJs routines.

Integration with IntroJs has been done for a lot of popular and famous frameworks. In this section, this topic will be discussed, and we will provide some extra description about the usage of IntroJs with other frameworks.

### Ruby on Rails

Ruby on Rails is one of the most popular frameworks for developing web applications. It is used by many developers, and it is easy to use IntroJs in Rails.

### Installation

There are a few simple steps for installing IntroJs in the Rails framework. First, install the IntroJs package using the following command:

**`gem install introjs-rails`**

You will then see the following output:

```
Fetching: sass-3.2.9.gem (100%)
Fetching: sass-rails-3.2.6.gem (100%)
Fetching: introjs-rails-0.4.0.gem (100%)
Fetching: activesupport-3.2.13.gem (100%)
Fetching: activemodel-3.2.13.gem (100%)
Fetching: rack-1.4.5.gem (100%)
Fetching: actionpack-3.2.13.gem (100%)
Successfully installed sass-3.2.9
Successfully installed sass-rails-3.2.6
Successfully installed introjs-rails-0.4.0
Successfully installed activesupport-3.2.13
Successfully installed activemodel-3.2.13
Successfully installed rack-1.4.5
Successfully installed actionpack-3.2.13
7 gems installed
Installing ri documentation for sass-3.2.9...
Installing ri documentation for sass-rails-3.2.6...
Installing ri documentation for introjs-rails-0.4.0...
Installing ri documentation for activesupport-3.2.13...
Installing ri documentation for activemodel-3.2.13...
Installing ri documentation for rack-1.4.5...
Installing ri documentation for actionpack-3.2.13...
Installing RDoc documentation for sass-3.2.9...
Installing RDoc documentation for sass-rails-3.2.6...
Installing RDoc documentation for introjs-rails-0.4.0...
Installing RDoc documentation for activesupport-3.2.13...
Installing RDoc documentation for activemodel-3.2.13...
Installing RDoc documentation for rack-1.4.5...
Installing RDoc documentation for actionpack-3.2.13...
```

The other way to do this task is by adding the `introjs-rails` package to your Gem file and installing the package using the `bundle install` command. You can find IntroJs Gem packages at `https://rubygems.org/gems/introjs-rails`.

After finishing the installation step, add the related files to your Rails project. Finally, add IntroJs resources to the code.

Add this line in `app/assets/javascript/application.js`:

```
//=require introjs
```

Also, add this line in `app/assets/stylesheets/application.css`:

```
*=require introjs
```

Now everything is ready for using the IntroJs library. All the IntroJs features that we mentioned before are accessible in your Rails project. Also, it is possible to update IntroJs after releasing new versions of the library.

## Yii Framework

Yii is one of the best frameworks for PHP. If you're using this framework, you can easily use benefits of integration of Yii and IntroJs.

### Installation

First, go to the `Yii-IntroJS` page on GitHub (`https://github.com/moein7tl/Yii-IntroJS`).

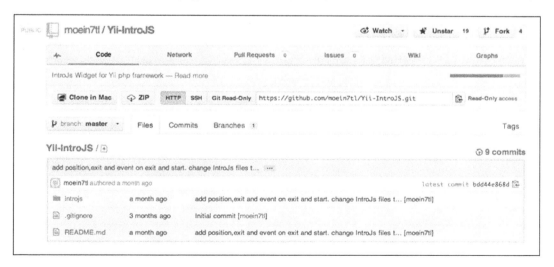

To download the compressed file, use the following link: `https://github.com/moein7tl/Yii-IntroJS/archive/master.zip`.

The .zip file includes the introjs directory, which should be copied in the protected path. Now, everything is ready to start.

## Usage

To use IntroJs, access application.extentions.introjs.IntroJs in the Yii project using the widget command. This widget gets an array, that is, all steps of the introduction, and generates the client-side code for the introduction automatically.

```
$this->widget('application.extensions.introjs.IntroJs',array(
    'data'=>array(
        array('id'=>'introID1','step'=>1,'intro'=>'Hello
World!','position'=>'right'),
        array('id'=>'IntroID2','step'=>2,'intro'=>'Step two'),
        /* all step and data should be defined here*/
        array('id'=>'introIDStart','start'=>true,'event'=>'onclick'),
// define one element as starter,default event is onclick
        array('id'=>'introIDExit','exit'=>true,'event'=>'onclick'), //
you can define elements to exit before ending IntroJs,default event is
onclick
    )
));
```

In this sample, we have defined two steps for introduction, including Hello World, and introID1 and introID2 as their IDs.

In each step, four identifiers can be defined:

✦ id: This defines each step's identity

✦ step: This determines each step's order

✦ intro: This determines each step's tool tip text

✦ position: This determines the tool tip's position. It can be top, right, bottom or left

In addition, this sample will to define two elements to start and finish the introduction; for example, it will to specify a link, which when clicked, starts or stops the introduction.

By setting the value of the start parameter to true, it is possible to start the custom element and determine an event for it; for example, the event can be onclick.

```
array('id'=>'introIDStart','start'=>true,'event'=>'onclick'), //
define one element as starter,default event is onclick
```

Also, by setting the exit parameter to true, it is possible to determine the exit element, for example:

```
array('id'=>'introIDExit','exit'=>true,'event'=>'onclick'), // you
can define elements to exit before ending IntroJs,default event is
onclickStyle Customization
```

By default, IntroJs has a simple style that can make a great harmony with your website design.

In this section, IntroJs styles will be explained, and the way to change the IntroJs elements' style and appearance will be learned.

To change IntroJs style, five main items should be changed. They are as follows:

+ Overlay
+ Tool tip
+ Buttons
+ Numbers
+ Highlight area

IntroJs has a stylesheet named `introjs.css` that was downloaded before. To change your introduction style, create a new CSS file and overwrite the `introjs.css` classes as you want. After that, include your own CSS file after the main CSS file in your page, as shown in the following example:

```
<!-- Add IntroJs styles -->
<link href="introjs.css" rel="stylesheet">
<!-- Here you should add your own style -->
<link href="mystyle.css" rel="stylesheet">
```

## Overlay

On opening the `introjs.css` file, the first available class is `introjs-overlay`, which includes all properties of the overlay. It is possible to overwrite properties in your own CSS file and change the overlay appearance.

## Tool tips

This is another important class in `introjs.css` is `introjs-tooltip` that includes all the properties of your introduction tool tips. For example, to change the tool tip's color to red, add the following code to the CSS file:

```
.introjs-tooltip {
    background-color: red;
}
```

## Buttons

It is also possible to change a button's style by overwriting a few classes.

### introjs-tooltipbuttons

`introjs-tooltipbuttons` is a class for a `div` element that is a `buttons` container. For example, to change the button's alignment to right, add the following code to the CSS file:

```
.introjs-tooltipbuttons {
    text-align: left;
}
```

### introjs-button

The `introjs-button` class includes all the appearance properties of buttons. The following example shows how to change some of them in the CSS file:

```
.introjs-button {
    text-shadow: 1px 1px 0 #fff;
    color: #333;
    background-color: #ececec;
    background-image: -webkit-gradient(linear, 0 0, 0 100%,
from(#f4f4f4), to(#ececec));
    background-image: -moz-linear-gradient(#f4f4f4, #ececec);
    background-image: -o-linear-gradient(#f4f4f4, #ececec);
    background-image: linear-gradient(#f4f4f4, #ececec);
}
.introjs-button {
    text-shadow: 1px 1px 0 #fff;
    font: 11px/normal sans-serif;
    color: #333;
    background-image: linear-gradient(#f4f4f4, #ececec);
}
```

### introjs-prevbutton

This class is for the **Previous** button.

### introjs-nextbutton

This class is for the **Next** button.

### introjs-skipbutton

This class is for the **Skip** button.

## Numbers

To change the style of the step number's CSS properties, which are in the `introjs-helperNumberLayer` class, overwrite this class in the CSS file.

## Highlight area

To change the highlight area's style, overwrite `introjs-helperLayerclass`.

# Localization and the Right to Left version

IntroJs gives a lot of functions and options to change and customize the library for the language that developers use. In IntroJs, some buttons and labels are available as options, and it is possible to alter them using IntroJs API and methods.

## Changing button labels

IntroJs has four buttons for various situations, and these buttons are in tool tip boxes. All these options could be changed via the `setOption` or `setOptions` method.

In order to change these buttons and set the preferred text, change the following options:

✦ `nextLabel`: This option is used to change the **Next** button's label

✦ `prevLabel`: This option is used to change the **Previous** button's label

✦ `skipLabel`: This option is used to change the **Skip** button's label

✦ `doneLabel`: This option is used to change the **Done** button's label

All the preceding options are changeable with the `setOption` method. The following is an example of using this function:

```
introJs().setOption("skipLabel", "Exit");
```

In the preceding example, we changed the **Skip** button label from **Skip** to `Exit`. With the same approach, change all the button's labels.

If you need to change two or more button's labels at once, use the `setOptions` method. An example of the `setOptions` method is as follows:

```
introJs().setOptions({ nextLabel: 'Go', prevLabel: 'Previous' });
```

In the previous example, we changed both the **Next** and **Previous** buttons' labels to Go and Previous using one function call. Finally, the result should be something like this:

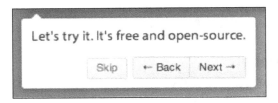

## RTL

IntroJs was released in the **Left to Right** version, but it is possible to update it to the **Right to Left** stylesheet. IntroJs has an **RTL** stylesheet to change the introduction to Right to Left, and it is easy to use this stylesheet.

To have the RTL version, add `introjs-rtl.css` to the page after the main IntroJs stylesheets. Be sure to use the RTL stylesheet after the main IntroJs stylesheets.

```
<!-- Add IntroJs styles -->
<link href="introjs.css" rel="stylesheet">
<!-- Add IntroJs RTL styles -->
<link href="introjs-rtl.css" rel="stylesheet">
```

After changing the page like we did in the preceding example, everything should be RTL, such as tool tip boxes and buttons. An example of the RTL version in action for the Persian language is as follows:

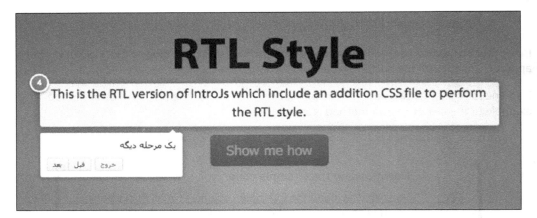

# Building projects

Sometimes a developer needs to change, develop, and customize IntroJs for his/her usage. For developing or customizing IntroJs, use the development files (the `intro.js` and `introjs.css` files) and after changing, prepare files for production use. It is possible to use development files for the production environment. All you need is to minify them and remove redundant comments and whitespaces.

The production environment is where your users will be and is the final release. Users don't like to waste their time on downloading files. Hence, minimize the size of the files as much as possible.

Creating the production code from development files is easy with IntroJs; all you need is to run a single line of command in your command-tools application. Then, `MakeFile` will manage everything to prepare and create production files. However, you need to prepare your workspace before running the commands.

## Getting ready

IntroJs `MakeFile` works with NodeJs, so before doing anything, if you don't have NodeJs, install it. You can use the following link to download NodeJs: `http://nodejs.org`; Select your operating system and download the installer file. After downloading it, run and install NodeJs. Now, you should have the NPM package manager in your system. To make sure the installation has been done correctly, open the command prompt, type the `npm` command, and press *Enter*. The **Node Package Manager** (**NPM**) manual will appear.

Now, everything is ready to go ahead. Open the command prompt and the folder of IntroJs, which has files as shown in the following screenshot:

```
Afshin-Mehrabanis-MacBook-Pro:usablica.intro.js afshinmehrabani$ ls -li
total 128
18174830 drwxr-xr-x  3 afshinmehrabani  staff    102 Jun 13 14:53 BUILD
18174832 -rw-r--r--  1 afshinmehrabani  staff     58 Jun 13 14:53 Makefile
18174833 -rw-r--r--  1 afshinmehrabani  staff   8813 Jun 13 14:53 README.md
18174834 -rw-r--r--  1 afshinmehrabani  staff    325 Jun 13 14:53 component.json
15594538 drwxr-xr-x  9 afshinmehrabani  staff    306 Jun 19 21:30 example
17460182 -rw-r--r--  1 afshinmehrabani  staff  24608 May 20 17:03 intro.js
18313076 -rw-r--r--  1 afshinmehrabani  staff    487 Jun 19 21:28 introjs-rtl.css
17460183 -rw-r--r--  1 afshinmehrabani  staff   6520 May 10 11:47 introjs.css
15594547 drwxr-xr-x  5 afshinmehrabani  staff    170 Jun 13 14:53 minified
18174853 -rw-r--r--  1 afshinmehrabani  staff    454 Jun 13 14:53 package.json
```

Install other dependencies to minify and compress CSS and JavaScript files. In the command prompt, type the npm install command and hit *Enter*; after a moment the result should appear, as shown in the following screenshot:

```
Afshin-Mehrabanis-MacBook-Pro:usablica.intro.js afshinmehrabani$ npm install
npm http GET https://registry.npmjs.org/node-minify
npm http 200 https://registry.npmjs.org/node-minify
npm http GET https://registry.npmjs.org/sqwish
npm http GET https://registry.npmjs.org/uglify-js
npm http 200 https://registry.npmjs.org/sqwish
npm http 200 https://registry.npmjs.org/uglify-js
npm http GET https://registry.npmjs.org/source-map
npm http GET https://registry.npmjs.org/optimist
npm http GET https://registry.npmjs.org/async
npm http 200 https://registry.npmjs.org/optimist
npm http 200 https://registry.npmjs.org/source-map
npm http GET https://registry.npmjs.org/source-map/-/source-map-0.1.23.tgz
npm http 200 https://registry.npmjs.org/source-map/-/source-map-0.1.23.tgz
npm http 200 https://registry.npmjs.org/async
npm http GET https://registry.npmjs.org/wordwrap
npm http GET https://registry.npmjs.org/amdefine
npm http 200 https://registry.npmjs.org/wordwrap
npm http 200 https://registry.npmjs.org/amdefine
node-minify@0.7.4 node_modules/node-minify
├── sqwish@0.2.1
└── uglify-js@2.3.6 (async@0.2.9, optimist@0.3.7, source-map@0.1.23)
```

As shown in the preceding screenshot, all the dependencies are installed automatically.

## make build

Run a command-line tool to create production code snippets. To do this, go to the folder of IntroJs and run the make build command. After running the command, a result as shown in the following screenshot will appear:

```
Afshin-Mehrabanis-MacBook-Pro:usablica.intro.js afshinmehrabani$ make build
cd BUILD && node BUILD.js
RTL CSS minified successfully.
Main CSS minified successfully.
JS minified successfully.
```

If the successful message from the application appears, it means that you have your production-ready files. All production files are stored in the `minified` folder inside the IntroJs folder. An example of the `minified` folder is as follows:

Also, production-ready files have the `.min` postfix in their filenames, which means minified. Now these files are ready for production in the minimum possible size.

## Events and callbacks

One of the most important part of IntroJs is its events and callbacks. There are various events that give a complete control of every part of the introduction. For example, it is possible to show a message at the end of the introduction. These events will improve in the forthcoming versions of IntroJs.

In this section, we'll explain some available events in IntroJs 0.4.0 (the last stable version at the time of writing this book).

### oncomplete

The `oncomplete` event happens when all introduction steps have been passed and the user reaches the last step. It is possible to access this event whenever the user presses the **Done** button or the right arrow key.

```
introJs().oncomplete(function() {
    alert("end of introduction");
});
```

This event doesn't pass any parameter to your callback function. In the callback function, `this` points to the current instance of `introJS`.

In the preceding example, the **end of introduction** message will appear after the introduction ends.

## onexit

`onexit` happens after the user exits from the introduction, which means that the user can exit from the whole event just before the introduction is completed by pressing the *Esc* button, or by clicking on the **Skip** button on the tool tip.

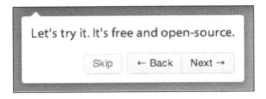

```
introJs().onexit(function() {
  alert("exit of introduction");
});
```

The callback method doesn't get any input parameter for this event. As the preceding example code indicates, the imported event doesn't have a parameter. Also in the callback method, the `this` value points to the current instance of `introJS`. Hence, it can be useful for controlling actions and also receiving more data for the introduction, which already has been launched on the page.

In the preceding example, as soon as the user exits from the introduction, the **exit of introduction** message will appear.

## onchange

After each level of introduction changes (by clicking on the **Next** or **Back** buttons in the tool tip panel or pressing right or left arrows on the keyboard), the `onchange` event happens. It can be useful whenever a developer wants to make a new action after the user enters one of the introduction's levels, such as calling a file as Ajax or to show data that had been read to the user.

```
introJs().onchange(function(targetElement) {
  alert("new step");
});
```

In the preceding event, the callback event receives an input parameter that includes the element while the introduction is running on it.

In the preceding code, the **new step** message pops up to the user after entering each level of the introduction.

## onbeforechange

Before entering a new level of the introduction, the `onbeforechange` event happens (just before the `onchange` event). Hence, it is useful to have an action just before the user enters a new level of the introduction, and after the action is finished, the new level will come up.

```
introJs().onbeforechange(function(targetElement) {
  alert("before new step");
});
```

In the callback event, one parameter is added; this includes an element that is placed by the introduction and the highlight area. Also, in the callback event, the `this` value points to the current `introJS` class' instance.

In the preceding example, before entering the new level of the introduction, the **before new step** message will pop up.

## Multipage introduction

In this section, multipaging, which is another important and interesting usage of IntroJs, that lets the developer learn how to create a multipage introduction, will be explained.

All the introductions you have made so far had a single page. However, how about having a multipage introduction instead of having all of them on a single page? What if you want to arrange the introduction's first three steps in `index1.html` and put the other parts in `index2.html`? Surely, there is no page count limit, and it is possible to divide the introduction as you like.

So, let's make a multipage introduction with two pages. To perform this action, we'll add a block of code to each page. Hence, add this code to the first page:

```
<script type="text/javascript">
document.getElementById('startButton').onclick = function() {
    //change doneLabel to "Next Page" instead of Done
introJs().setOption('doneLabel', 'Next page').start().
oncomplete(function() {
    //redirect to next page
window.location.href = 'second.html?multipage=true';
        });
    };
</script>
```

Then in the second page, add this code:

```
<script type="text/javascript">
    //start introJs if multipage parameter is passed on the url
if (RegExp('multipage', 'gi').test(window.location.search)) {
introJs().start();
    }
</script>
```

# How it works

As it indicates, to make the introduction multipage, two blocks of code snippets have been added. But how does it work? Let us go through it in this section.

### Changing the Done button label

On the first page, change the **Done** button label as a first step. It notifies the user that the introduction hasn't finished yet, and it will continue to the next page.

### Redirecting the user to the next page

As it is explained before, it is possible to use the `oncomplete` event to notify when the introduction finishes. Also, this event happens at the end of introduction, and we can make a decision at that time.

To make a multipage introduction, we should transfer the user to the next page in `oncomplete`. For this action, change `window.location.href`. Remember that we set `multipage` to `true` as a query string parameter. This parameter will also be used in the second page.

```
window.location.href = 'second.html?multipage=true';
```

### Starting the introduction on the second page

After redirecting to the second page, the introduction should continue and call the `introjs.start()` method from IntroJs. The `multipage` parameter will be set to `true`. If the `multipage` parameter exists, we call `introjs.start()` and the introduction will continue.

Be careful about the introduction steps. The order of the `data-step` values in all the pages should be correct. For example, if the last number in the first page is 4, the first number in the second page should be 5.

# People and places you should get to know

Here you can find some good places to get information about the latest versions of IntroJs, news, and updates.

## IntroJs official website

The official IntroJs website includes download links, the API documentation, blogs, and other interesting resources. The link is as follows: `http://introjs.com`.

## Blogs

This is a great place to find latest news about the project. Also, this is where the IntroJs development team post updates and future plans. The link is as follows: `http://blog.introjs.com`.

## API documentation

Find the complete API documentation of IntroJs at `http://introjs.com/api`.

## The GitHub repository

GitHub is the code repository of IntroJs. Find the last stable version to download at `https://github.com/usablica/intro.js/`.

## Issue tracker

People write their issues, problems, and their own ideas about different projects here. Other development teams and contributors check the issues to fix them. The link is as follows: `https://github.com/usablica/intro.js/issues`.

## Communities

There are several places that you can refer to in order to discuss IntroJs.

### Google group

A group for people to discuss IntroJs is as follows: `https://groups.google.com/forum/#!forum/introjs`.

### Stackoverflow

Questions and discussions on IntroJs in Stackoverflow are done here, which are labeled with the `#introjs` tag: `http://stackoverflow.com/questions/tagged/intro.js`.

## Twitter and personal blogs

Afshin Mehrabani's (the main developer of IntroJs and a co-founder of Usablica) Twitter profile and personal blog URLs are as follows:

+ `http://twitter.com/afshinmeh`
+ `http://afshinm.name/`

Ehsan Arasteh's (a contributor to various versions of IntroJs and the CEO of Usablica) Twitter profile and personal blog URLs are as follows:

+ `http://twitter.com/ehsandotnet`
+ `http://blog.ehsandotnet.me`

Usablica's (an individual team that IntroJs and many other open source projects and startups make under its brand) Twitter profile and blog URLs are as follows:

+ `http://twitter.com/usablica`
+ `http://usabli.ca/`

**Thank you for buying**
# Instant IntroJs

## About Packt Publishing

Packt, pronounced 'packed', published its first book "*Mastering phpMyAdmin for Effective MySQL Management*" in April 2004 and subsequently continued to specialize in publishing highly focused books on specific technologies and solutions.

Our books and publications share the experiences of your fellow IT professionals in adapting and customizing today's systems, applications, and frameworks. Our solution based books give you the knowledge and power to customize the software and technologies you're using to get the job done. Packt books are more specific and less general than the IT books you have seen in the past. Our unique business model allows us to bring you more focused information, giving you more of what you need to know, and less of what you don't.

Packt is a modern, yet unique publishing company, which focuses on producing quality, cutting-edge books for communities of developers, administrators, and newbies alike. For more information, please visit our website: www.packtpub.com.

## Writing for Packt

We welcome all inquiries from people who are interested in authoring. Book proposals should be sent to author@packtpub.com. If your book idea is still at an early stage and you would like to discuss it first before writing a formal book proposal, contact us; one of our commissioning editors will get in touch with you.

We're not just looking for published authors; if you have strong technical skills but no writing experience, our experienced editors can help you develop a writing career, or simply get some additional reward for your expertise.

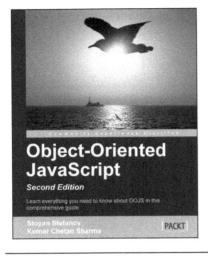

## Object-Oriented JavaScript - Second Edition

ISBN: 978-1-84969-312-7          Paperback: 382 pages

Learn everything you need to know about OOJS in this comprehensive guide

1.  Think in JavaScript

2.  Make object-oriented programming accessible and understandable to web developers

3.  Apply design patterns to solve JavaScript coding problems

4.  Learn coding patterns that unleash the unique power of the language

## Social Data Visualization with HTML5 and JavaScript

ISBN: 978-1-78216-654-2          Paperback: 107 pages

Leverage the power of HTML5 and JavaScript to build compelling visualizations of social data from Twitter, Facebook, and more

1.  Learn how to use JavaScript to create compelling visualizations of social data

2.  Use the d3 library to create impressive SVGs

3.  Master OAuth and how to authenticate with social media sites

Please check **www.PacktPub.com** for information on our titles

**Developing Windows Store Apps**
**with HTML5 and JavaScript**

## Developing Windows Store Apps with HTML5 and JavaScript

ISBN: 978-1-84968-710-2    Paperback: 184 pages

Learn the key concepts of developing Windows Store apps using HTML5 and JavaScript

1. Learn about the powerful new features in HTML5 and CSS3

2. Quick start a JavaScript app from scratch

3. Get your app into the store and learn how to add authentication

**Drupal 6 JavaScript and jQuery**

## Drupal 6 JavaScript and jQuery

ISBN: 978-1-84719-616-3    Paperback: 340 pages

Putting jQuery, AJAX, and JavaScript effects into your Drupal 6 modules and themes

1. Learn about JavaScript support in Drupal 6

2. Packed with example code ready for you to use

3. Harness the popular jQuery library to enhance your Drupal sites

4. Make the most of Drupal's built-in JavaScript libraries

Please check **www.PacktPub.com** for information on our titles

www.ingramcontent.com/pod-product-compliance
Lightning Source LLC
Chambersburg PA
CBHW060445060326
40690CB00019B/4338